Meeting
Christ
Now

GOD OUR KING

Teach me, my God and King
In all things thee to see;
And what I do in anything
To do it as for thee.

George Herbert

Meeting Christ Now

*Prayer and the Sacraments
for Young People*

DAVID KONSTANT

AND

WINIFRED WILSON RSCJ

Photographs by Noeline Kelly
Illustrations by Ann-Marie Stuart

COLLINS

Collins Liturgical Publications
187 Piccadilly, London W1V 9DA

Concordat cum originali
and Nihil obstat: John P. Dewis
Imprimatur: David Norris
Westminster, 25th June 1976

First Published 1976
© 1976 text and illustrations Collins Publishers

Made and printed in Great Britain
by William Collins Son & Co. Ltd, Glasgow

CONTENTS

Acknowledgements

English translation of the Roman Missal, Rite of Baptism for Children, Rite of Confirmation, Rite of Penance, copyright © 1969, 1970, 1972, 1973, 1974, 1975, International Committee on English in the Liturgy, Inc. All rights reserved.
Extracts from scripture from the Jerusalem Bible version of scripture, © 1966, 1967 and 1968, Darton, Longman & Todd, and Doubleday & Co Inc.

Readings: The publishers acknowledge with thanks permission to use the following copyright texts in the section of readings:
Jonathan Cape Ltd, and Mr F. R. Fletcher, editor, for the extract from Kilvert's Diary; and Chris Searle, editor of *Fire Words*, for the following poems: Timmy Crow, 'The Chance', Sally Beale, 'Old Age', Mark Vinten, 'My Parents'.
Darton, Longman & Todd, for extract from *Rule for a New Brother*.
Ginn & Company Ltd, and Leslie Scadding, for the poem 'My Hand', from *Mirror Poems*.
The Grail (England) for extracts from *The Psalms: A New Translation*, © The Grail (England) 1953 and published by Collins in Fontana Books.
MacGibbon & Kee, Granada Publishing, for e. e. cummings, 'i thank You God for this most amazing'.
Macmillan London and Basingstoke, for extract from William Temple, *Readings in St John's Gospel*; and for 'Tortoise's Prayer', from *Prayers from the Ark*, by Carmen Bernos de Gasztold, trans. by Rumer Godden.
Oxford University Press and Alan T. Dale, for extracts from *New World* and *Winding Quest*.
Paulist Press and Huub Oosterhuis, for Indian Prayer from *Open Your Hearts*; and François Chagneau, for lines from *Stay with Us*.
G. T. Sassoon, for Siegfried Sassoon, for 'A flower has opened'.

INTRODUCTION

This is a book for you to *use* rather than to read. What you find in it will depend on who you are and what you are looking for. It is something like a treasure chest full of different jewels – this gem will appeal to one person and that one to another. Or you can think of it as a larder stocked with different foods – some of them you want today, others will take your fancy tomorrow, and there are certain basic things like bread that you may need every day. So perhaps you can dip into this as you might into a treasure chest, or take what is necessary, as you would from your own larder.

The purpose of the book is to help you to know God, to talk with him and to hear him. God is with us and cares for us all the time: 'He's got the whole world in his hands.' He speaks to us as we go about our day-to-day work and play; we speak to him by the way we live as well as when we take time off to pray. But there are certain highlights in our conversation with God. There are some especially important moments in our lives when we know that God is deeply present to us. Among these moments are the celebrations of God's presence that we call sacraments. What is written here is to help you think and pray about some of these moments – your baptism and your confirmation, your celebrations of the eucharist and of forgiveness, so that you may grow closer to God and to your fellow men and women.

David Konstant   Winifred Wilson

PRAYER

The apostles saw Jesus praying and said to him: 'Lord, teach us to pray.'

Jesus was often seen to pray. Occasionally he spent the whole night in prayer. He prayed at all the great moments of his life: before he began his public work; before he chose his friends, the apostles; before the Transfiguration; after the feeding of the five thousand; at the Last Supper; during his agony in the garden of Gethsemane. But, in a very real way, the whole of his life was a prayer, because he was so close to God his Father. He described this closeness when he said, 'I and the Father are one.'

This was the secret that the apostles stumbled on – that prayer is being close to God and then expressing this closeness in some way. Another word for being close to God like Jesus was is 'communion'.

Have you ever watched how people in love talk to each other? Sometimes they talk quite ordinarily about day-to-day things; at other times they talk just about the special things which interest them; there will be times when they ask each other for advice or help or comfort; they will often have occasion to thank each other; they will tell each other how happy they are to be together; at times they will not talk at all, just be silent in each other's company – a look or a gesture or a single word is enough to express all they want to say to each other. However they show it, it is obvious that they care for each other, have faith in each other, enjoy each other's company, and are happy and content to be together. They are in 'communion' with each other.

When we pray we are trying to say to God all that is really important to us; and we are trying to grow closer to him. Like the apostles we often say, 'Lord, teach us to pray.'

Jesus's first lesson in prayer was to teach them the *Our Father*. This prayer puts into a very few words the things we want to say to God.

First, we call God '*Father*'. He is indeed our creator, the all-powerful one; but the wonderful thing is that he is completely fatherly towards us: generous, loving, forgiving, strong, protective, caring.

'*Hallowed be thy name*': we pray that all creation may recognize the holiness of God, and that the kingdom Jesus came to preach may really come to pass.

'*Thy will be done*' – we pray that good will overcome evil.

'*Give us this day our daily bread*' – very basic words, in which we ask for all we need for life.

'*Forgive us . . . as we forgive*' – we ask our Father to help us live as the Gospel teaches us, treating others as we wish to be dealt with ourselves.

'*Lead us not into temptation . . .*' – we ask for guidance in the difficult choices that face us every day.

Jesus gave some other advice about prayer.

'Don't babble', he said. 'Ask and you shall receive.' Ask, and go on asking; before you pray, forgive those who have hurt you; pray quietly in your room, in private.

The word GOSPEL gives a pattern to remind us of some helpful things about prayer.

Prayer is

G   being with **G**od and talking with him.

O   being **O**pen with God, so as to change our way of life.

S   being **S**ilent and **S**incere. God knows us through and through. We don't have to be always talking. And when we do talk, our words must be real, we must mean what we say.

P   God being **P**resent to us, and we being in his **P**resence.

E   about **E**veryday things – the things that are important to us.

L   **L**istening *to* God, **L**istening *for* God. We shall not hear a voice speaking inside us, but if we learn to listen we shall know from time to time that God has spoken. Sometimes he speaks through other people, or through things that happen, or in our inner thoughts – but in the end he always speaks.

Everyone learns to pray in his own way. In the end the only way you can learn is from you and God working together.

We give the collection of prayers that follows just to help you find God for yourself. Use what you find useful, and don't be afraid to talk with God, face to face, in your own words. Learn from this prayer from the psalms:

BE STILL AND KNOW THAT I AM GOD.

THE PRAYER JESUS TAUGHT US

Our Father, who art in heaven,
hallowed be thy name;
thy kingdom come;
thy will be done
on earth as it is in heaven;
give us this day our daily bread,
and forgive us our trespasses
as we forgive those who trespass against us;
and lead us not into temptation,
but deliver us from evil.   Amen.

See Matthew 6:9-13

SOME OTHER PRAYERS WE KNOW JESUS SAID

Father, I thank you for hearing my prayer.

At the raising of Lazarus, John 11:41

Father, everything is possible for you. Take this cup away from me.
But let it be as you, not I, would have it.

At his agony in the garden. Mark 14:36

Father, forgive them; they do not know what they are doing.   *As he hung on the cross. Luke 23:34*

THE CANTICLE OF MARY (THE MAGNIFICAT)

This is the song of joy Mary sang when the angel announced to her that she would bear the Christ. See Luke 1:46-55.

My soul glorifies the Lord,
my spirit rejoices in God, my Saviour.

He looks on his servant in her lowliness;
henceforth all ages will call me blessed.

The Almighty works marvels for me.
Holy his name!
His mercy is from age to age,
on those who fear him.

He puts forth his arm in strength
and scatters the proud-hearted.
He casts the mighty from their thrones
and raises the lowly.

He fills the starving with good things,
sends the rich away empty.

He protects Israel, his servant,
remembering his mercy,
the mercy promised to our fathers,
to Abraham and his sons for ever.

THE HAIL MARY

Christians have used this prayer since the eleventh century. Its first two lines are the greeting used by the angel when he came to tell Mary that God had chosen her to bear the Christ (see Luke 1:29). Lines 3 and 4 are the words of Elizabeth, mother of John the Baptist, to Mary (see Luke 1:42).

Hail Mary, full of grace, the Lord is with you.
Blessed are you among women,
and blessed is the fruit of your womb, Jesus.
Holy Mary, mother of God, pray for us sinners
now and at the hour of our death.   Amen.

IN PRAISE OF THE HOLY TRINITY

This short song of praise fixes our prayer on the nature of God, the eternal Trinity. It has been used as a prayer-ending since earliest Christian times.

> Glory be to the Father,
> and to the Son,
> and to the Holy Spirit;
> as it was in the beginning
> is now, and ever shall be,
> world without end.   Amen.

THE APOSTLES' CREED

A personal statement of faith that has been used especially at baptisms, since the early Church.

I believe in God, the Father almighty,
creator of heaven and earth;
and in Jesus Christ, his only Son, our Lord;
who was conceived by the Holy Spirit,
born of the Virgin Mary,
suffered under Pontius Pilate,
was crucified, died and was buried.
He descended into hell;
the third day he rose again from the dead.
He ascended into heaven
and sits at the right hand of God, the almighty Father.
From thence he will come to judge the living and the dead.
I believe in the Holy Spirit;
the holy catholic Church;
the communion of saints;
the forgiveness of sins;
the resurrection of the body;
and the life everlasting.   Amen.

PRAYER

OUT OF THE DEPTHS – A CRY FOR FORGIVENESS

Out of the depths I cry to you, O Lord,
Lord, hear my voice!
O let your ears be attentive
to the voice of my pleading.

If you, O Lord, should mark our guilt,
Lord, who would survive?
But with you is found forgiveness:
for this we revere you.

My soul is waiting for the Lord,
I count on his word.
My soul is longing for the Lord
more than watchman for daybreak.

Because with the Lord there is mercy
and fullness of redemption,
his people indeed he will redeem
from all their iniquity.   *From Psalm 129*

Jesus, son of David, have mercy on me.
          The prayer of the blind man, Luke 18:38

SOME PRAYERS OF THE SAINTS
WHO WERE GOD'S FRIENDS IN TIMES PAST

THE PRAYER OF ST BERNARD (THE MEMORARE)

Remember, O most loving Virgin Mary,
that it has never been heard of
for anyone to fly to your protection,
implore your help,

or seek your intercession,
and be left forsaken.
Therefore, filled with confidence in your goodness,
I fly to you, O mother, Virgin of Virgins.
I come to you, I stand before you,
a sorrowful sinner.
Do not despise my words, O mother of the Word,
but graciously hear and grant my prayer.

THE PRAYER OF ST BENEDICT

O gracious and holy Father,
give us wisdom to perceive you,
intelligence to understand you,
diligence to seek you,
patience to wait for you,
eyes to behold you,
a heart to meditate upon you,
and a life to proclaim you;
through the power of the Spirit
of Jesus Christ our Lord.

THE PRAYER OF ST RICHARD

Thanks be to you, my Lord Jesus Christ,
for all the benefits which you have given me,
for all the pains and insults
which you have borne for me:
O most merciful Redeemer, Friend and Brother,
may I know you more clearly,
love you more dearly,
follow you more nearly,
day by day.

THE PRAYER OF ST IGNATIUS

Teach us, good Lord,
to serve you as you deserve;
to give and not to count the cost,
to fight and not to heed the wounds,
to toil and not to seek for rest,
to labour and not to ask for any reward,
save that of knowing that we do your will;
through Jesus Christ our Lord.

THE PRAYER OF ST PATRICK

I bind unto myself today
the power of God to hold and lead:
his eye to watch, his might to say,
his ear to hearken to my need;
the wisdom of my God to teach,
his hand to guide, his shield to ward;
the Word of God to give me speech,
his heavenly host to be my guard.

Christ be with me, Christ within me,
Christ behind me, Christ before me,
Christ beside me, Christ to win me,
Christ to comfort and restore me.
Christ beneath me, Christ above me,
Christ in quiet, Christ in danger,
Christ in hearts of all that love me,
Christ in mouth of friend and stranger.

THE PRAYER OF ST FRANCIS

Lord, make me an instrument of your peace.
Where there is hatred, let me sow love;
where there is injury, pardon;
where there is discord, union;
where there is doubt, faith;
where there is despair, hope;
where there is darkness, light;
where there is sadness, joy.

O divine Master,
grant that we may not so much seek
to be consoled as to console;

to be understood as to understand;
to be loved as to love;
through the love of your Son who died for us,
Jesus Christ our Lord.

THE ANGELUS

A prayer in which we meditate on the fact that God became man for our sakes. It may be said three times a day: early morning, noon, and evening.

The angel of the Lord declared to Mary.
And she conceived of the Holy Spirit.   Hail Mary . . .

Behold the handmaid of the Lord.
Be it done to me according to your word.   Hail Mary . . .

The Word was made flesh,
and dwelt among us.   Hail Mary . . .

Pray for us, O holy Mother of God,
that we may be made worthy of the promises of Christ.

Let us pray: Pour forth, we beseech you, O Lord, your grace into our hearts, that we, to whom the incarnation of Christ your Son was made known by the message of an angel, may by his passion and cross be brought to the glory of his resurrection, through the same Christ our Lord.   Amen.

A PRAYER TO OUR LADY

Mary, you are God's mother and our mother also.
You and Joseph cared for your son Jesus when he was
    young.

You taught him to walk, to talk, and to pray.
You were anxious like any mother as he grew to manhood.
Help us, Mary, by your prayers;
help us to trust in God;
help us to pray to God our Father,
united in the love of the Holy Spirit
with Jesus Christ, your Son.

A MORNING PRAYER

> Lord God,
> you have given us a new day.
> Give us grace today to work for your glory,
> and for our neighbours' good;
> so that all we do and say,
> and think and pray,
> may make this day a perfect gift.

Let us bless our Saviour, who by his rising to new life
has freed the world from fear.
℟ Lord, lead us to the truth.

Lord Jesus, as this day begins, we remember that you are
the risen Christ, and therefore we look to the future with
confidence. ℟

We offer you our prayer this morning; take to yourself
our cares, our hopes and our needs. ℟

Deepen in us our love for you today, so that in all things
we find our good, and the good of others. ℟

Lord Jesus, we pray that through our own troubles we
may learn to feel the sufferings of others; help us to show
them your compassion. ℟

AN EVENING PRAYER

Lord Jesus Christ,
gentle and strong of heart;
accept we pray all we have done today,
and give us the rest we need
so that we may be ever more willing
to serve you and our fellow men.

May the Lord support us all the day long,
till the shades lengthen and the evening comes,
and the busy world is hushed,
and the fever of life is over,
and our work is done.
Then in his mercy
may he give us a safe lodging,
and a holy rest,
and peace at the last. Amen.

J. H. Newman

Save us, Lord, while we are awake;
protect us while we sleep;
that we may keep watch with Christ
and rest with him in peace.

The Lord grant us a quiet night and a perfect end. Amen.
From Night Prayer, in The Divine Office

A PRAYER FOR COURAGE

Lord God, our Father,
send us your Spirit,
so that we may find the strength and courage
to do what we know is right.

A PRAYER FOR FAMILY AND FRIENDS

One of your gifts to us, Father,
is the love of our families and friends.
Keep them close to you and give them all they need;
increase their joys,
comfort them if they are unhappy,
strengthen them if they find life hard.
Teach us to be grateful to them for all they do for us,
and help us to return their love.

A PRAYER FOR THE SICK

We know, Lord God, that you have a special love for
    the sick.
They are your children and they are in pain.
Give them the courage to accept their sickness.
Help them to discover a value in suffering.
In your good time bring them true relief.
Keep them content, happy and peaceful.

A PRAYER FOR THOSE WHO HAVE DIED

We pray, Father,
that one day we shall make our home with you in your
    kingdom.
We now ask you to care for those who have already died,
especially for . . .
May they be at peace in heaven with you.
May they be united by the love of the Holy Spirit,
in the brotherhood of your Son and of all the saints.

Just before he died himself, Jesus said:
'Do not let your hearts be troubled.
Trust in God still, and trust in me.

There are many rooms in my Father's house;
I am going now to prepare a place for you.'

John 14:1-2

The thief, hanging on the cross, said: 'Lord, remember
me when you come into your kindgom.'

'Indeed, I promise you,' Jesus replied, 'today you will
be with me in paradise.'

Luke 23:42-3

Sacraments of Initiation
BAPTISM AND
CONFIRMATION

We know we are with God when we recognize the signs of his presence. There are many signs of God's presence among us: the world we live in; the people we know and love; our prayer and our work – all these can speak to us of the 'wonderful works of God'. The greatest sign that God is with us is Jesus Christ, who was born in Palestine, lived there, died, and rose from the dead, and now lives among us.

In the sacraments, we meet Jesus. He is no longer among us in the way he was present to his friends when he lived in Galilee. But, on the night before he died, during his last meal with his friends, he said that he would ask God the Father to send them the Spirit, his own Spirit who would be with them for ever. This Holy Spirit, whom the Father continues to send, is the presence of Jesus. The sign (or sacrament) of his presence among us now is the Church – the body of believers to which we belong.

The word 'sacrament' comes from the Greek word for 'mystery'. It means something rich and hidden which reveals itself little by little to those who believe. A sacrament uses a familiar, everyday thing or event (like water, oil, bread, forgiveness) to make real for us the presence of Jesus. When we celebrate a sacrament, these familiar things bring us to a true meeting with Jesus Christ, and so lead us with the Spirit to the Father.

BAPTISM

When someone is baptized, Christ is inviting that person to belong to the Church. A young child cannot know what is happening, and is too young to accept the invitation on his own account. So his parents and godparents accept the invitation for him.

Infant baptisms usually take place on a Sunday, the day when the Church specially celebrates the resurrection of Jesus Christ. Friends and neighbours of the family, and the people of the parish, should be present as representatives of the whole Church. They welcome the new member of the Church, share the parents' joy, join in making the act of faith on the child's behalf, and accept by their presence some responsibility for the child's growth as a Christian. Gradually the child grows up, and becomes independent, and as he does so he is able to respond personally more and more deeply to Christ's invitation.

An adult who asks to be baptized is making a real and personal response to Christ's invitation. He or she has chosen to follow Christ and to make a sign of this by joining Christ's Church. By choosing to be baptized he declares his faith in Jesus Christ and promises to try to live up to his teaching. But an adult (like a child) has to grow in faith and goodness, so he also needs the support and friendship of godparents, neighbours and friends. In the early days of the Church adults were baptized after a long period of preparation (called the *catechumenate*) during the Easter Vigil. This meant that they became full members of the Church and made their first Communion on the great feast of the Christian year – Easter Sunday, the day of the Lord's Resurrection. This is once again becoming a fairly common practice in the Church. (If a non-Catholic Christian who has already been baptized wishes to join the Catholic Church he takes part in a special ceremony of welcome called the Reception of a Convert. There is, of course, no need for him to be baptized again.)

A baptism really is a true celebration, and there should be a birthday spirit about the occasion. The person being baptized is joyfully proclaimed a child of God the Father, a brother or sister of Christ, and a member of the people of God, the Church. He becomes a Christian, in other words is anointed with the Spirit (the word 'Christ' means 'anointed').

The ceremony described below refers to the baptism of a child; when an adult is baptized there are certain differences in the rite.

RECEPTION OF THE CHILDREN

At the beginning of the ceremony, the priest greets the parents and godparents who are waiting with the child at the entrance of the church. Their entry into the building is a sign of the child's entry into the communion of saints.

Priest What name do you give your child?
Parents say the name given (N.)
Priest What do you ask of God's Church for N.?
Parents say in their own words what they are seeking:
  e.g. Baptism, *or* faith, *or* eternal life *or* the life of Christ *or* the gift of the Holy Spirit.
Priest says something like this:
  You have asked for your child to be baptized . . . It will be your duty to bring him up to keep God's commandments as Christ taught us, by loving God and our neighbour . . .
Priest says to the child:
  N., the Christian community welcomes you with great

26

joy. In its name I claim you for Christ our Saviour by the sign of his cross. I now trace the cross on your forehead, and invite your parents and godparents to do the same.

Parents and godparents make the sign of the cross on the baby's forehead.

CELEBRATION OF GOD'S WORD

Then there is a short Liturgy of the Word. The Gospel is read, there is a homily, and the Prayer of the Faithful. These prayers ask God to bless the child who is being brought into the Church; to give him the faith to be a witness to the gospel; to bring him happiness. There is a prayer for the parents and godparents, that by their example they may teach the child what a Christian life means. The final prayer is for all those present, asking God to renew the grace of their baptism. Then the prayers of the whole of the Church are asked for in a short litany.

PRAYER OF EXORCISM AND ANOINTING BEFORE BAPTISM

Every baby is born as a member of the sinful human race, and needs to be set free from slavery to sin. In baptism he is born again, given the new life of Christ. Now he is a member of a redeemed race, the Church. This is expressed in a prayer like the following:

Almighty God,
you sent your only Son to rescue us from the slavery
    of sin,
and to give us the freedom
only your sons and daughters enjoy.

We now pray for this child
who will have to face the world with its temptations,
and fight the devil in all his cunning.

Your Son died and rose again to save us.
By his victory over sin and death,
bring this child out of the power of darkness.
Strengthen him with the grace of Christ,
and watch over him at every step in life's journey.
We ask this through Christ our Lord.   *All*   **Amen.**

BLESSING OF BAPTISMAL WATER

The priest then calls down God's blessing on the water that will be used for the baptism. The prayer begins:

Father, you give us grace through sacramental signs, which tell us of the wonders of your unseen power.

In baptism we use your gift of water . . .

Then, after referring to the saving power of water in the events of the Old and New Testament, it ends:

By the power of the Spirit give to the water of this font the grace of your Son.

You created man in your own likeness: cleanse him from sin in a new birth to innocence by water and the Spirit.

We ask you, Father, with your Son to send the Holy Spirit upon the water of this font. May all who are buried with Christ in the death of baptism rise also with him to newness of life.

RENUNCIATION OF SIN AND PROFESSION OF FAITH

Parents and godparents then speak for the child. On his behalf they renounce sin and evil, and proclaim their faith in God and in the Church. (If you want to see what they actually say, turn to p. 35, and see the 'Renewal of Baptismal Promises' in the Rite of Confirmation.)

The priest then says:

This is our faith. This is the faith of the Church. We are proud to profess it, in Christ Jesus our Lord.

And all reply: **Amen.**

The family brings the child to the font. The priest asks parents and godparents:

Is it your will that N. should be baptized in the faith of the Church, which we have all professed with you?

Parents and godparents: **It is.**

The priest baptizes the child, saying as he pours the water or immerses the child three times:

N., I baptize you in the name of the Father,
and of the Son,
and of the Holy Spirit.

Three symbolic actions follow: anointing with chrism; clothing with a white garment; handing over a lighted candle.

ANOINTING WITH CHRISM

Chrism is oil mixed with perfume – the oil signifies strength, the perfume is a sign of the good example that the Christian life should be to others. As the priest anoints the child, he prays:

God the Father of our Lord Jesus Christ has freed you from sin, given you a new birth by water and the Holy Spirit, and welcomed you into his holy people. He now anoints you with the chrism of salvation. As Christ was anointed Priest, Prophet, and King, so may you live always as a member of his body, sharing everlasting life.

CLOTHING WITH WHITE GARMENT

The white garment is a sign of the innocence and dignity of the newly-born Christian. The priest gives it to the child and says:

N., you have become a new creation, and have clothed yourself in Christ. See in this white garment the outward sign of your Christian dignity. With your family and friends to help you by word and example, bring that dignity unstained into the everlasting life of heaven.

LIGHTED CANDLE

The candle is the sign of Christ, the light of the world. Every year at Easter a special candle is blessed to symbolize the presence of Christ to us throughout the year. The Easter Candle has been burning throughout the baptism service. Now small candles are lighted from it, and given to the parents and godparents, as the priest says:

Parents and godparents, this light is entrusted to you to be kept burning brightly. This child of yours has been enlightened by Christ. He is to walk always as a child of the light. May he keep the flame of faith alive in his heart. When the Lord comes, may he go out to meet him with all the saints in the heavenly kingdom.

Everyone says the Lord's Prayer together, and the ceremony ends with a final prayer and blessing by the priest.
A song may be sung at the end of the ceremony.

CONFIRMATION

Confirmation is the occasion when, in the presence of the bishop and the people of your parish, you freely and on your own account make the promises that were made for you at baptism. It is an important stage in your life as a Christian. It completes your entry into the community of the Church.

At baptism, you were passive, unaware. You received God's gift, but you were incapable of responding to it. Nonetheless, through the faith of your parents and godparents who answered for you, God's love and life took possession of your being.

Now you have reached an age when you can make an active, conscious response to God's gift of his life and love. You yourself can say the promises that were made for you at baptism, and mean them.

Already you have been trying to live as a Christian. You know that the Spirit of Jesus is within you. The Spirit leads you to see more clearly what is right and good, he helps you to be more aware of the times when you are selfish, unkind, untruthful, when you fall below the ideal Jesus puts before you. You are realizing more strongly that you do have the power to choose between what is good and what is not good. You know what it is to pray, to speak in your own words to God, who loves you and forgives you, to tell him about anything that concerns you – happy or sad or puzzling or depressing. You know, too, what it is to be silent in the presence of God so that he can speak to you.

At confirmation, the Church recognizes you as a full member. You, on your part, accept that this means that you must live out the promises made for you in baptism. Confirmation completes your baptism. You have already been admitted to the Holy Eucharist, and these three sacraments together make up your 'initiation' into the Church.

We read in the Acts of the Apostles how the apostles, as Jesus had promised, received the Holy Spirit and were given

the power to share this gift with others (Acts 2:1-4). St Paul laid his hands on those who had already been baptized, and the Holy Spirit came to them (Acts 19:1-6). At confirmation, the bishop, who is the successor of the apostles, gives the Holy Spirit to you so as to complete your baptism.

Confirmation makes you more like Jesus, who was anointed by the Holy Spirit at his baptism in the Jordan. Like him you will be invited to share in the work of the Spirit. Your work will be to bring joy, peace, contentment and love into people's lives, so as to build up the body of Christ, the Church, and to make the world a better place to live in. As a confirmed Christian you are called on to serve all mankind.

Confirmation is usually celebrated during Mass. The Mass begins in the normal way. After the readings, the bishop speaks to those who are to be confirmed about the meaning of the sacrament. Then they renew the promises made when they were baptised.

RENEWAL OF BAPTISMAL PROMISES

The bishop questions the candidates:

Bishop   Do you reject Satan and all his works and all his empty promises?

Candidate   **I do.**

Bishop   Do you believe in God, the Father almighty, creator of heaven and earth?

Candidate **I do.**

Bishop Do you believe in Jesus Christ, his only Son, our Lord,
who was born of the Virgin Mary,
was crucified, died and was buried,
rose from the dead,
and is now seated at the right hand of the Father?

Candidate **I do.**

Bishop Do you believe in the Holy Spirit,
the Lord, the giver of life,
who came upon the apostles at Pentecost
and today is given to you sacramentally in confirmation?

Candidate **I do.**

Bishop Do you believe in the holy catholic Church,
the communion of saints, the forgiveness of sins,
the resurrection of the body, and life everlasting?

Candidate **I do.**

The bishop confirms this profession of faith by proclaiming the faith of the Church:

This is our faith. This is the faith of the Church.
We are proud to profess it in Christ Jesus our Lord.

The whole congregation responds: **Amen.**

THE LAYING ON OF HANDS

The bishop stands with joined hands, facing the people, and says:

My dear friends:
in baptism God our Father gave the new birth of
  eternal life
to his chosen sons and daughters.
Let us pray to our Father
that he will pour out the Holy Spirit
to strengthen his sons and daughters with his gifts
and anoint them to be more like Christ the Son of God.

All pray in silence for a short time.
*The bishop and the priests who will minister the sacrament with
him lay hands upon all the candidates (by extending their hands
over them). The bishop alone sings or says:*

All-powerful God, Father of our Lord Jesus Christ,
by water and the Holy Spirit
you freed your sons and daughters from sin
and gave them new life.
Send your Holy Spirit upon them
to be their Helper and Guide.
Give them the spirit of wisdom and understanding,
the spirit of right judgment and courage,
the spirit of knowledge and reverence.
Fill them with the spirit of wonder and awe in your
  presence.
We ask this through Christ our Lord.
All **Amen.**

THE ANOINTING WITH CHRISM

The apostles gave the Holy Spirit to those they confirmed by laying their hands on them. The bishop does this by the imposition of hands and the anointing of the candidate's forehead with chrism. This action, together with the words, 'Be sealed with the Gift of the Holy Spirit' is the sacramental sign. The oil signifies strength; the perfume reminds us that our behaviour towards others should attract them to the following of Christ and that this is part of our spreading of the Good News, the Gospel of Christ.

The bishop dips his right thumb in the chrism and makes the sign of the cross on the forehead of the one to be confirmed, as he says:

N., be sealed with the Gift of the Holy Spirit.

The newly confirmed replies: **Amen.**

Bishop Peace be with you.

The newly confirmed replies: **And also with you.**

PRAYER OF THE FAITHFUL

Bishop My dear friends:
     let us be one in prayer to God our Father
     as we are one in the faith, hope, and love his Spirit gives.

Deacon or
minister For these sons and daughters of God,
     confirmed by the gift of the Spirit,
     that they may give witness to Christ
     by lives built on faith and love:
     let us pray to the Lord.
     All **Lord, hear our prayer.**

Deacon or minister For their parents and godparents
who led them in faith,
that by word and example they may always encourage
them
to follow the way of Jesus Christ:
let us pray to the Lord.
All **Lord, hear our prayer.**

Deacon or minister For the holy Church of God,
in union with N. our pope, N. our bishop, and all the
bishops,
that God, who gathers us together by the Holy Spirit,
may help us grow in unity of faith and love
until his Son returns in glory:
let us pray to the Lord.
All **Lord, hear our prayer.**

Deacon or minister For all men,
of every race and nation,
that they may acknowledge the one God as Father,
and in the bond of common brotherhood
seek his kingdom,
which is peace and joy in the Holy Spirit:
let us pray to the Lord.
All **Lord, hear our prayer.**

Bishop God our Father,
you sent your Holy Spirit upon the apostles,
and through them and their successors
you give the Spirit to your people.
May his work begun at Pentecost
continue to grow in the hearts of all who believe.
We ask this through Christ our Lord.   *All*   **Amen.**

LITURGY OF THE EUCHARIST

The liturgy of the eucharist is now celebrated, see p. 54.

THE BLESSING

At the end of Mass, the Bishop gives this special blessing to the people present:

Bishop God our Father
   made you his children by water and the Holy Spirit:
   may he bless you
   and watch over you with his fatherly love. *All* **Amen.**

Bishop Jesus Christ the Son of God
   promised that the Spirit of Truth
   would be with his Church for ever:
   may he bless you and give you courage
   in professing the true faith.   *All* **Amen.**

Bishop The Holy Spirit
   came down upon the disciples
   and set their hearts on fire with love:
   may he bless you,
   keep you one in faith and love
   and bring you to the joy of God's kingdom.

All **Amen.**

Bishop May almighty God bless you,
   the Father, and the Son, and the Holy Spirit.

All **Amen.**

The ceremony ends with the sign of the cross, the same sign that was placed on the forehead of those confirmed. That sign was a seal. A seal on a document testifies that it is genuine; the sign of the cross on the forehead testifies that the candidate is one of Christ's followers. This seal lasts for ever.

THE EUCHARIST

THE CELEBRATION OF MASS

The Mass is the great Christian prayer. It is a prayer of both words and actions.

Every year, the Jews eat a meal called the Paschal or Passover meal, in remembrance of the day when they were set free from Egypt where they had been slaves. You can read the story of their escape from Egypt in the Old Testament, in the Book of Exodus, chapters 12-15. On the evening of Maundy Thursday, the day before he died, Jesus Christ ate the Paschal Meal with his friends the apostles. But he did not just do what was always done at the Passover meal; he did something new.

Towards the end of the meal, he took bread, gave thanks, and said:

'This is my body, given for you.' Then he took a cup of wine and said: 'This is my blood which is shed for you. Do this in memory of me.' He gave the bread and wine to his friends, who ate and drank. In giving them this food and drink he gave them his very self. This was the first Mass.

Ever since then, Christians have done what Christ asked when he said: 'Do this in memory of me.' We provide the bread and wine, gifts of our earth, for this sacrificial meal. Through God's power, given to the priest who in the name of Christ says: 'This is my body', 'This is my blood', Christ is made present in these gifts: Jesus Christ, who gave his body to be broken, his blood to be shed, who loved us to the end, and who was raised from death by his Father. He does all this for us, that we may live with his life now and for ever. So at this moment we shout out or sing an acclamation, such as

'Christ has died, Christ is risen, Christ will come again.'

At Mass, then, the sacrifice of Christ's love is made present to us again. Like the apostles we are invited to share in it. This is a new Paschal meal, which is celebrated not just once a year in Jerusalem, but every day throughout the whole world. It is a celebration that, like all the sacraments, brings Christ to us in a special way. We call our share in the celebration our 'communion' because when we receive Christ we are joined to him and to all other Christians.

But to share is to give, as well as to receive. When we receive Christ in communion we, too, are asked to give something. We promise to try to love others; to be at peace with one another; to live for others; to share our goods with others freely and cheerfully; to be happy and content with others; to take on the job which God has given us; to get to know God better. In short, we promise that we will try to love God and our fellow-men without any selfishness. If we can love like that, our lives, like Christ's, will be a sacrifice. Our celebration of Mass is a prayer that above everything else draws us close to God and to each other. Let us celebrate happily, eagerly and sincerely.

What do we do at Mass?

It may be helpful to think of the Mass in five stages, like this:

Come We come together, as God's family, ask forgiveness for our sins, praise his glory and tell him our needs.

Listen We listen to the readings from the Bible, and to the priest who talks to us about the Good News of our salvation. We may all say together the creed, We believe . . .

Give Thanks We bring our gifts of bread and wine, and in a great prayer of thanksgiving, we ask God to accept these gifts so that they may become for us the body and blood of his Son Jesus. We call to mind all that God has done for us.

Take and Eat We receive communion, and at one with our Lord, we pray together in peace and thankfulness.

Go We are sent out into the world with a blessing, to do God's work.

THE ORDER OF MASS

THE PREPARATION: COME!

ENTRANCE

As the priest comes to the altar we may sing a hymn or say together the Entrance Antiphon for the day. We then make the sign of the cross as the priest says:

Priest   In the name of the Father, and of the Son and of the Holy Spirit.
People   **Amen.**

The priest greets us in one of the following ways, or in similar words:
<1
Priest   The grace of our Lord Jesus Christ and the love of God and the fellowship of the Holy Spirit be with you all.
People   **And also with you.**

<2
Priest   The grace and peace of God our Father and the Lord Jesus Christ be with you.
People   **Blessed be God, the Father of our Lord Jesus Christ.**
< *or*
People   **And also with you.**

<3
Priest   The Lord be with you.
People   **And also with you.**

THE PENITENTIAL RITE

The priest may say a few words about the Mass of the day.
He then invites us to repentance in one of the following ways,
or in similar words:

<1

Priest My brothers and sisters,
   to prepare ourselves to celebrate the sacred mysteries,
   let us call to mind our sins.
After a brief silence, all say:

All **I confess to almighty God,**
   and to you, my brothers and sisters,
   that I have sinned through my own fault,
All strike their breast
   in my thoughts and in my words,
   in what I have done,
   and in what I have failed to do;
   and I ask blessed Mary, ever virgin,
   all the angels and saints,
   and you, my brothers and sisters,
   to pray for me to the Lord our God.
The Absolution follows; see page 46.

<2

Priest My brothers and sisters,
   to prepare ourselves to celebrate the sacred mysteries,
   let us call to mind our sins.

After a brief silence, the priest says:
   Lord, we have sinned against you:
   Lord, have mercy.
People **Lord, have mercy.**

Priest Lord, show us your mercy and love.
People **And grant us your salvation.**
The Absolution follows; see below.

<3
Priest My brothers and sisters,
  to prepare ourselves to celebrate the sacred mysteries,
  let us call to mind our sins.

*After a brief silence, the priest says the following, or uses similar
words. Our response, however, remains the same:*

Priest You were sent to heal the contrite:
  Lord, have mercy.
People **Lord, have mercy.**

Priest You came to call sinners:
  Christ, have mercy.
People **Christ, have mercy.**

Priest You plead for us at the right hand of the Father:
  Lord, have mercy.
People **Lord, have mercy.**

THE ABSOLUTION

Priest May almighty God have mercy on us,
  forgive us our sins,
  and bring us to everlasting life.
People **Amen.**

A PRAYER FOR MERCY

*We now ask Jesus, who is Lord and Christ, to have mercy on us.
(This prayer is not said if the third form of the Penitential Rite
has been used.)*

Priest   Lord, have mercy.
People   **Lord, have mercy.**
Priest   Christ, have mercy.
People   **Christ, have mercy.**
Priest   Lord, have mercy.
People   **Lord, have mercy.**

THE GLORIA

*On certain days we say or sing the hymn of praise which begins
with the words the angel sang to the shepherds on the first Christmas
day.*

**Glory to God in the highest,
  and peace to his people on earth.**

**Lord God, heavenly King,
almighty God and Father,
  we worship you, we give you thanks,
  we praise you for your glory.
Lord Jesus Christ, only Son of the Father,
Lord God, Lamb of God,
you take away the sin of the world:
  have mercy on us;
you are seated at the right hand of the Father:
  receive our prayer.**

**For you alone are the Holy One,
you alone are the Lord,
you alone are the Most High,
  Jesus Christ,
  with the Holy Spirit,
  in the glory of God the Father. Amen,**

THE OPENING PRAYER

Priest   Let us pray.

There is a short pause now to let us talk to God quietly. Then the priest says the prayer for today's Mass. At the end of this we answer: **Amen.**

THE LITURGY OF THE WORD: LISTEN!

THE READINGS

We listen to the readings from the Bible. When the Bible is read to us, God is speaking to his people through his word.
God speaks. We listen.
The first one or two readings will come from the Old Testament, or from the book called the Acts of the Apostles, the story of the early days of the Church, or from a letter written by one of the apostles. At the end of the first two readings, the reader says:

Reader   This is the Word of the Lord.
People   **Thanks be to God.**

A Psalm follows the first reading. It is like a meditation on the reading we have just heard. Make the response, which we all say, your own prayer in answer to the message of the reading.
We all stand to greet the Gospel, in which Christ speaks to us. We sing the Alleluia verse to welcome Christ who brings us the Good News. Then the priest says:
Priest   The Lord be with you.
People   **And also with you.**
Priest   A reading from the holy Gospel according to N.
People   **Glory to you, Lord.**

We listen to the Gospel, in which the life, works and words of Jesus our Lord are told to us. At the end of the Gospel reading, the priest says:

Priest This is the gospel of the Lord.

People **Praise to you, Lord Jesus Christ.**

THE HOMILY

After the Gospel, the priest will probably say a few words to us, to help us understand the Gospel, and learn what it can mean for us in our daily lives.

THE PROFESSION OF FAITH

We may stand, and all together publicly affirm our faith by saying the We believe. *When the celebration is for children, the Apostles' Creed on page 14, may be said:*

We believe in one God,
   the Father, the Almighty,
   maker of heaven and earth.
   of all that is, seen and unseen.

We believe in one Lord, Jesus Christ,
   the only Son of God,
   eternally begotten of the Father,
   God from God, Light from Light,
   true God from true God,
   begotten, not made,
   of one Being with the Father.
   Through him all things were made.
   For us men and for our salvation
     he came down from heaven:
All bow their heads
   by the power of the Holy Spirit
   he became incarnate from the Virgin Mary, and
     was made man.

For our sake he was crucified under Pontius Pilate;
   he suffered death and was buried.
   On the third day he rose again
     in accordance with the Scriptures;
   he ascended into heaven
     and is seated at the right hand of the Father.
   He will come again in glory to judge the living
     and the dead,
   and his kingdom will have no end.

We believe in the Holy Spirit, the Lord, the giver of
    life,
  who proceeds from the Father and the Son.
  With the Father and the Son he is worshipped
    and glorified.
  He has spoken through the Prophets.
  We believe in one holy catholic and apostolic
    Church.
  We acknowledge one baptism for the forgiveness
    of sins.
  We look for the resurrection of the dead,
    and the life of the world to come. Amen.

THE PRAYER OF THE FAITHFUL

*When we celebrate Mass we pray for our own needs, for the needs
of those we know and love, and for the needs of all men. Before
our gifts of bread and wine are brought to the altar, we gather
our requests in some short prayers (sometimes called the Bidding
Prayers). The prayers vary according to the needs of the moment.
First there is an invitation to prayer, then the Bidding Prayers
follow. The people make a response to each prayer. At the end,
the priest gathers our petitions into a final prayer, to which we
all reply:* **Amen.**

THE LITURGY OF THE EUCHARIST: GIVE THANKS!

THE OFFERING OF BREAD AND WINE

The bread and wine which is to be used for the sacrifice is brought to the altar and is given to God. The gift is a simple one – food and drink. (We may also bring other gifts as well – samples of our work, offerings of our money.)

In making this present to God we are showing that all we have comes from God and especially life itself. God will accept our gift and change it so that it becomes Christ himself. The offering of the bread and wine is a sign that we want to make a present of our lives, today and always.

While the gifts are brought to the altar, we may sing a song of offering.

The priest takes the bread and says:

Priest   Blessed are you, Lord, God of all creation.

Through your goodness we have this bread to offer,
which earth has given and human hands have made.
It will become for us the bread of life.

People   **Blessed be God for ever.**

While he is pouring wine and a little water into the chalice the priest says quietly:

Priest   By the mystery of this water and wine
may we come to share in the divinity of Christ,
who humbled himself to share in our humanity.

Then the priest takes the chalice and says:

Priest   Blessed are you, Lord, God of all creation.

Through your goodness we have this wine to offer,
fruit of the vine and work of human hands.
It will become our spiritual drink.

People   **Blessed be God for ever.**

The priest bows and says quietly:
Priest Lord God,
   we ask you to receive us
   and be pleased with the sacrifice we offer you
   with humble and contrite hearts.

As he washes his hands the priest says to himself:
   Lord, wash away my iniquity; cleanse me from my sin.

He then invites us all to pray:
Priest Pray, brethren, that our sacrifice*
   may be acceptable to God, the almighty Father.
People **May the Lord accept the sacrifice at your
   hands,**
   for the praise and glory of his name,
   for our good, and the good of all his Church.

*The priest now says the Prayer over the Gifts for today's Mass.
At the end we answer:* **Amen.**

THE EUCHARISTIC PRAYER

*Now begins the great prayer of thanks during which our gifts
become the body and blood of Christ. There are a number of
these prayers. The one which follows here is Eucharistic Prayer II.
The priest may begin by reminding us of the particular reasons
for our celebration of Mass today. He then says:*

* (In England and Wales): my sacrifice and yours

53

Priest   The Lord be with you.
People   **And also with you.**
Priest   Lift up your hearts.
People   **We lift them up to the Lord.**
Priest   Let us give thanks to the Lord our God.
People   **It is right to give him thanks and praise.**

THE PREFACE

There are a large number of prayers which introduce the Eucharistic Prayer. These introductory prayers are called Prefaces; they remind us in a formal way of the reasons for which we give God thanks and praise. The one which follows belongs with Eucharistic Prayer II:

Father, it is our duty and our salvation,
always and everywhere
to give you thanks
through your beloved Son, Jesus Christ.

He is the Word through whom you made the universe,
the Saviour you sent to redeem us.
By the power of the Holy Spirit
he took flesh and was born of the Virgin Mary.

For our sake he opened his arms on the cross;
he put an end to death
and revealed the resurrection.
In this he fulfilled your will
and won for you a holy people.

And so we join the angels and the saints
in proclaiming your glory
as we say (sing):

All **Holy, holy, holy Lord, God of power and might,**
heaven and earth are full of your glory.
  Hosanna in the highest.

Blessed is he who comes in the name of the Lord.
Hosanna in the highest.

The priest continues alone.

THE BLESSING OF THE BREAD AND WINE

Lord, you are holy indeed,
the fountain of all holiness.
Let your Spirit come upon these gifts
to make them holy,
so that they may become for us
the body and blood of our Lord, Jesus Christ.

THE CONSECRATION

*Now takes place what happened at the Last Supper; the priest
does and says what our Lord did and said.*

Before he was given up to death,
a death he freely accepted,
he took bread and gave you thanks.
He broke the bread,
gave it to his disciples, and said:
Take this, all of you, and eat it:
this is my body which will be given up for you.

When supper was ended, he took the cup.
Again he gave you thanks and praise,
gave the cup to his disciples, and said:
Take this, all of you, and drink from it:
this is the cup of my blood,
the blood of the new and everlasting covenant.
It will be shed for you and for all men
so that sins may be forgiven.
Do this in memory of me.

THE ACCLAMATION

Priest Let us proclaim the mystery of faith:

*The celebration of the Eucharist is a celebration of the life,
death and resurrection of Christ; it is a mystery, in other words
a deep sign from which we can always grasp a richer meaning;
it is an act of faith, by which we declare ourselves as followers of
Christ. We reply to the priest's invitation:*

<1   **Christ has died,
       Christ is risen,
       Christ will come again.**

<2   **Dying you destroyed our death,
       rising you restored our life.
       Lord Jesus, come in glory.**

<3   **When we eat this bread and drink this cup,
       we proclaim your death, Lord Jesus,
       until you come in glory.**

<4   **Lord, by your cross and resurrection
       you have set us free.
       You are the Saviour of the world.**

A PRAYER TO THE FATHER

In memory of his death and resurrection,
we offer you, Father, this life-giving bread, this saving cup.
We thank you for counting us worthy
to stand in your presence and serve you.

A PRAYER FOR UNITY

May all of us who share
in the body and blood of Christ
be brought together in unity by the Holy Spirit.

A PRAYER FOR THE CHURCH

Lord, remember your Church throughout the world;
make us grow in love,
together with N. our Pope,
N. our bishop, and all the clergy.

A PRAYER FOR THE DEAD

Remember our brothers and sisters
who have gone to their rest
in the hope of rising again;
bring them and all the departed
into the light of your presence.

A PRAYER FOR OURSELVES

Have mercy on us all;
make us worthy to share eternal life
with Mary, the virgin mother of God,
with the apostles, and with all the saints
who have done your will throughout the ages.
May we praise you in union with them,
and give you glory
through your Son, Jesus Christ.

IN PRAISE OF GOD

Through him,
with him,
in him,
in the unity of the Holy Spirit,
all glory and honour is yours,
almighty Father,
for ever and ever.
All **AMEN.**

THE COMMUNION RITE:
TAKE AND EAT!

We have made the gift of ourselves to God, and the bread and wine are now Christ himself. Now we prepare ourselves for our share in the sacred meal.

THE LORD'S PRAYER

We all say together the prayer of God's family, the prayer Christ taught us. We all acknowledge God as our Father, we pray for his kingdom; we pray for our daily needs and for forgiveness of our sins. The priest invites us to join in this prayer in these or similar words:

Priest Let us pray with confidence to the Father
in the words our Saviour gave us:
All **Our Father, who art in heaven,
hallowed be thy name.
Thy kingdom come.
Thy will be done on earth, as it is in heaven.**

Give us this day our daily bread,
and forgive us our trespasses,
as we forgive those who trespass against us.
And lead us not into temptation,
but deliver us from evil.

Priest   Deliver us, Lord, from every evil,
and grant us peace in our day.
In your mercy keep us free from sin
and protect us from all anxiety
as we wait in joyful hope
for the coming of our Saviour, Jesus Christ.

People   **For the kingdom, the power, and the glory**
are yours,
now and for ever.

PRAYER FOR PEACE

Priest   Lord Jesus Christ,
you said to your apostles:
I leave you peace, my peace I give you.
Look not on our sins, but on the faith of your Church,
and grant us the peace and unity of your kingdom
where you live for ever and ever.

People   **Amen.**

Priest   The peace of the Lord be with you always.

People   **And also with you.**

On some occasions the priest will invite us to greet each other,
saying: Let us offer each other the sign of peace.
We then make a sign of peace, according to local custom.

THE BREAKING OF THE BREAD

The priest breaks the host, puts a piece of it into the chalice and quietly prays that those who receive the living Christ may share his life. He says:

May this mingling of the body and blood
of our Lord Jesus Christ
bring eternal life to us who receive it.

The breaking of the host is like the breaking of bread at a meal; it is a sign that we are all soon to share in the sacramental meal of Christ's body and blood. During the breaking of the bread we all say:

**Lamb of God, you take away the sins of the world:
have mercy on us.
Lamb of God, you take away the sins of the world:
have mercy on us.
Lamb of God, you take away the sins of the world:
grant us peace.**

PRAYER BEFORE COMMUNION

The priest says quietly one of the two following prayers.

Priest Lord Jesus Christ, Son of the living God,
by the will of the Father and the work of the Holy Spirit
your death brought life to the world.
By your holy body and blood
free me from all my sins and from every evil,
keep me faithful to your teaching,
and never let me be parted from you.

< or
Priest   Lord Jesus Christ,
   with faith in your love and mercy
   I eat your body and drink your blood.
   Let it not bring me condemnation
   but health in mind and body.

COMMUNION

The priest holds up the host and says:

Priest   This is the Lamb of God
   who takes away the sins of the world.
   Happy are those who are called to his supper.
All   **Lord, I am not worthy to receive you,**
   but only say the word and I shall be healed.

Before the priest receives the consecrated bread and wine he says quietly:
   May the body of Christ bring me to everlasting life.
and
   May the blood of Christ bring me to everlasting life.

When we go to the altar to receive communion the priest says:

Priest   The body of Christ.

and we answer: **Amen.**

*In receiving Christ we are united with him and with each other.
When we have sung the communion hymn we can talk quietly to
God for a few moments. We can thank him for everything he
has given us – life, parents, friends, happiness. We can ask him
for all our needs, though we must be willing to accept whatever
he gives us. We can talk to him about our sorrows and dis-
appointments, our joys and hopes; about our relatives, friends
and companions; about our day-to-day life. All that interests us
interests him because we are his children.
After a pause for silent prayer the priest says:*

    Let us pray.

*He then says the Prayer after Communion for the day, at the
end of which we answer:* **Amen.**

*If there are any announcements to be made they should follow
now.*

CONCLUDING RITE: GO!

THE BLESSING

*Before we leave the altar to carry on with our daily jobs, the
priest blesses us and sends us out in God's name; we make the
sign of the cross together with him, which sets a seal on what we
have been doing together as Christians at the altar.*

Priest   The Lord be with you.
People **And also with you.**
Priest   May almighty God bless you,
   the Father, and the Son, and the Holy Spirit.
People **Amen.**

The priest sends us out into the world, saying:

Priest The Mass is ended, go in peace.
or Go in the peace of Christ.
or Go in peace to love and serve the Lord.
People **Thanks be to God.**

As the priest leaves the altar we may sing a hymn of praise and thanks.

THE SACRAMENT OF PENANCE

SIN AND FORGIVENESS

All of us act in ways we know are wrong. We fall short of what is ideal. Even though we want to avoid sin, it is always a struggle to be completely true to our conscience. We sin when we say to ourselves: 'I don't care what's right, or what

God wants me to do – I'm going to do this.' Sin is turning away from God and from our conscience, and acting selfishly. A person can turn totally away and so cut himself off from God completely. But surely this is very rare, and requires great deliberation and malice. Most people try to lead good lives; their failures do not separate them from God, but weaken their relationship with him.

There are many ways in which we accept God's forgiveness: when we sincerely take part in the penitential act at the beginning of Mass; when we receive Holy Communion; when we pray for forgiveness; when we forgive others; and more solemnly and clearly when we celebrate the sacrament of penance.

The sacrament of penance is a sure sign that we are forgiven by God and are accepted by his people, the Church. It is a means of repairing and strengthening our relationship with God and our fellow men. Here are some important things to think about:

● God always loves me; he does not change his attitude towards me because I sin.

● I am forgiven when I turn back to God and accept his love; the celebration of the sacrament of penance bears witness to his love and acceptance of me.

● I belong to the community of the Church; when I sin I show my weakness and, in however slight a way, harm this community; the sacrament of penance is a sign that this community, the Church, accepts me and wants to help me.

● Before I can truly celebrate the sacrament of penance I must practise forgiveness in my daily life: 'Forgive us our trespasses as we forgive those who trespass against us.'

● When I celebrate this sacrament and accept God's forgiving love, I accept all that goes along with this: 'If you love me,' says Christ 'keep my commandments.'

A SERVICE OF PENANCE

What follows may be of help to an individual preparing for the sacrament of penance, or to a group that wants to celebrate a service of penance – though as far as possible, a group should prepare its own service of penance. The prayers and readings suggested are by way of example.

A PRAYER FOR FORGIVENESS

O God,
you search me and you know me,
you know me through and through;
you know my weaknesses and my difficulties,
my failures and my struggles.
Send me your Spirit
so that I may have the strength
to follow where you call
and to be obedient to your will.
Make me a true disciple
of your Son, Jesus Christ our Lord.

A READING

The sacrament of penance, like all the sacraments, is a meeting with Christ, whom St John calls 'the Word of God'. It is helpful to read or listen to the Word of God from the scriptures so as to appreciate better the forgiving love of the Father.

The Reading is from St Paul's letter to the Romans

I cannot understand my own behaviour. I fail to carry out the things I want to do, and I find myself doing the very things I hate. When I act against my own will, that means that I have a self that acknowledges that the Law is good, and so the thing behaving in that way is not my self but sin living in me. The fact is, I know of nothing good living in me – living that is in my unspiritual self, for though the will to do what is good is in me, the performance is not, with the result that instead of doing the good things I want to do, I carry out the sinful things I do not want. When I act against my will, then, it is not my true self doing it, but sin which lives in me.

What a wretched man I am! Who will rescue me from this body doomed to death? Thanks be to God through Jesus Christ our Lord! The reason why those who are in Christ Jesus are not condemned, is that the law of the spirit of life in Christ Jesus has set you free from the law of sin and death. *Romans 7:14-20. 24-5. 8:1*

Other readings which may be appropriate are Psalm 139 (p. 91), Luke 15:11-32 (the prodigal son), Luke 22:31-34, 54-62 and John 21:15-19 (Peter's denial and forgiveness), Luke 23:39-43 (the penitent thief).

REFLECTION

One or more of the following ideas may help you to understand what the Word of God is saying:

● The road to freedom is a long and hard one; I become more and more free as I learn to overcome my weaknesses.

● I cannot overcome sin on my own; I need the help and support of my fellow-men and of God, who is a Father to me.

● I have a duty to help and forgive others, just as they have a duty to help and forgive me.

● God loves me and accepts me just as I am; I need never be afraid that he will reject me.

● Whatever my sinfulness, my sorrow wins immediate forgiveness.

● I am not wholly master of myself; there will always be an inward struggle between my conscience (what I know is right) and my will (what I want to do); yet there is nothing that can separate me from the love of Christ.

AN EXAMINATION OF CONSCIENCE

If you are to turn back to God you need to reflect on the ways you have turned away from him, and on the ideals of the life of the Christian. As a baptized follower of Christ, you are sealed with the Spirit and are invited to live according to the Spirit. St Paul sums up this life in one short sentence (Galatians 5:23):

What the Spirit brings is: love, joy, peace, patience, kindness, goodness, trustfulness, gentleness and self-control.

You can use this sentence as a guide, to see how closely you manage to follow Christ. Do not necessarily use all of what follows for your examination of conscience; in any case, the questions only suggest the direction in which to look – there may be one particular direction that you know you ought specially to think about. At a service of penance those taking part should prepare a group examination of conscience, allowing a pause for reflection after each question.

love *Love of God* – how do I show it . . . by prayer . . . by my faith and hope . . . by my actions? . . .
love of others – of my parents . . . of my brothers and sisters . . . of my friends . . . of those I work with . . . of those in other parts of the world . . . is my love just words, or do I show it by what I do? . . .
love of myself – it is right to love myself, but am I selfish . . . or proud . . . or jealous . . . or envious . . . or mean? . . .
love of things – Jesus said, 'No man can serve two masters, God and money'; do I consider money more important than anything else . . . am I greedy about what I have . . . do I share with others? . . .

joy Do I try to spread joy and happiness . . . am I surly, or bad-tempered, or irritable, or miserable . . . do I complain a lot . . . do I make other people angry or unhappy by my attitude? . . .

peace Do I try to live at peace with others and to make peace between others . . . am I at peace in myself . . . do I fight or contradict or quarrel . . . am I a good loser . . . am I prepared to accept law and authority? . . .

patience Am I impatient with myself (or with others) . . . do I expect too much of myself (or of others) . . . do I accept myself (or others) . . . do I get upset if things don't go my way . . . do I want quick and easy results, without bothering to work? . . .

kindness Am I thoughtful for other people . . . for my family . . . for those who are tired after a busy day . . . for those who clear up after me . . . for the rest of those in the queue . . . for the sick and handicapped . . . for the one who has been left out of things? . . .

goodness Is my religion just a matter of going to Church, . . . am I generous in the help I give to others . . . do I put a limit to my goodness . . . am I afraid to do what I ought because of what my friends will say . . . do I admire and try to copy the goodness of others? . . .

trustfulness Am I trustworthy . . . do I trust others . . . do I let my friends down . . . do I tell the truth . . . am I sincere in what I do . . . do I do what I am asked or told to do, with reluctance or willingly . . . do I help to build up trust in the groups I belong to? . . .

gentleness Do I try to get my way by force . . . am I violent in speech . . . do I hurt others by my words or actions . . . do I regard gentleness as a sign of weakness . . . do I use my authority justly and with gentleness . . . how do I react when others are violent with me . . . do I respect the dignity of others in the way I treat them? . . .

self-control Do I try to control my mind, my actions, and my emotions . . . do I try to acquire worthwhile habits . . . do I waste my time day-dreaming . . . do I take proper care of my health . . . do I waste food and drink through greed . . . do I treat myself with dignity . . . do I use my gifts and talents properly? . . .

AN ACT OF REPENTANCE

Jesus Christ is our saviour; he saves us from slavery to sin and shows us how to be truly free. Now you have thought about your way of life, and about your weaknesses and failures, turn to our Lord in sorrow, and ask him to lead you to make a practical and helpful resolution.

> I confess to almighty God,
> and to you, my brothers and sisters,
> that I have sinned through my own fault,
> in my thoughts and in my words,
> in what I have done,
> and in what I have failed to do;
> and I ask blessed Mary, ever virgin,
> all the angels and saints,
> and you, my brothers and sisters,
> to pray for me to the Lord our God.

During a service of penance a short litany such as the following can be prepared by the group:

Give us the grace of true sorrow for our sins.
    ℟. **Have mercy, Lord, and hear us.**
Forgive us our failures and encourage us to persevere.
    ℟. **Have mercy, Lord, and hear us.**
Help us to know our weaknesses so that we may learn to overcome them.
    ℟. **Have mercy, Lord, and hear us.**
Teach us to be forgiving and tolerant towards each other.   ℟. **Have mercy, Lord, and hear us.**
Make us true disciples of your Son, and servants of each other.   ℟. **Have mercy, Lord, and hear us.**
Let us now pray to God for his understanding and forgiving mercy, in the words of his Son, Jesus Christ:
    Our Father . . .

CONFESSION AND ABSOLUTION

When, either in a group or alone, you have prepared yourself to celebrate the sacrament of penance, you may ask a priest to hear your confession and give you absolution. This is a very personal sacrament, so although there is a simple pattern you can follow, this is only as a guide, to help you; what is important is to speak and pray from the heart. The priest is there as your friend and counsellor; to receive your confession of faith and sorrow on behalf of the Church; and in the name of the Church to declare your forgiveness by God and your full reconciliation to your fellow-men. Even if on some occasion a priest is unhelpful or unsympathetic, try not to be put off or afraid. Remember our Lord's words: 'Come to me all you who labour and are heavily burdened, and I will refresh you.' This sacrament can bring a wonderful sense of peace and tranquillity.

Begin by making the sign of the cross as you say the simple prayer which reminds you that you are always in God's hands:

> In the name of the Father,
> and of the Son,
> and of the Holy Spirit. Amen.

Then tell the priest when you last celebrated the sacrament, so far as you can remember.

The priest may then read to you a short passage from scripture or a prayer to remind you of God's love, and to invite you to sorrow. Here are some examples:

> <1 The Lord does not wish the sinner to die
>   but to turn back to him and live.
>   Come before him with trust in his mercy.
> > *Ezekiel 33:11*

> <2 May the Lord Jesus welcome you.
>   He came to call sinners, not the just.
>   Have confidence in him. *Luke 5:32*

> <3 May the grace of the Holy Spirit
>   fill your heart with light,
>   that you may confess your sins with loving trust
>   and come to know that God is merciful.

> <4 May the Lord be in your heart
>   and help you to confess your sins with true sorrow.

*Then, in any way you like, perhaps with the help of the priest,
confess your sins. Talk about your struggles and your difficulties,
your efforts and your failures. Ask for any help and advice you
may need.*

*When your confession is complete the priest will give you a
penance (a prayer, an act of self-denial, or an act of service to
others) to help you start afresh and to overcome your weaknesses.*

*He will then invite you to express your sorrow and your will-
ingness to make amends in a prayer asking for God's forgiveness.
Here are some examples:*

<1 Remember, Lord, your compassion and mercy which
you showed long ago.
Do not recall the sins and failings of my youth.
In your mercy remember me, Lord, because of your
goodness.   *Psalm 24:6-7*

<2 Lord, I am sorry and ask for forgiveness for my sins.
With your help I will try not to sin again.

<3 Lord Jesus, Son of God, have mercy on me, a sinner.

<4 Lamb of God, you take away the sins of the world:
have mercy on me.

<5 Lord, I am not worthy of your love,
but say only a word, and I shall be healed.

*After this prayer the priest will make the sign of the cross and
say the words of absolution:*
Priest   God, the Father of mercies,
through the death and resurrection of his Son
has reconciled the world to himself

and sent the Holy Spirit among us
for the forgiveness of sins;
through the ministry of the Church
may God give you pardon and peace,
and I absolve you from your sins
in the name of the Father, and of the Son, ✠
and of the Holy Spirit.
Penitent **Amen.**

Then the priest will send you on your way with one of the following prayers:

<1 *Priest* Give thanks to the Lord, for he is good.
Penitent **His mercy endures for ever.**
Priest The Lord has freed you from your sins. Go in peace.

<2 May the Passion of our Lord Jesus Christ,
the intercession of the Blessed Virgin Mary and of all
the saints,
whatever good you do and suffering you endure,
heal your sins,
help you to grow in holiness,
and reward you with eternal life.
Go in peace.

<3 The Lord has freed you from sin.
May he bring you safely to his kingdom in heaven.
Glory to him for ever.
Penitent **Amen.**

<4 Blessed are those
whose sins have been forgiven,
whose evil deeds have been forgotten.
Rejoice in the Lord,
and go in peace.

<5 Go in peace,
and proclaim to the world
the wonderful works of God,
who has brought you salvation.

The final words, 'Go in peace' remind us that when our Lord spoke to the apostles about the forgiveness of sin his opening words, repeated a few moments later, were 'Peace be with you.' You have now celebrated God's forgiving love and are invited to share your new-found peace with others. The sacrament does not end with the absolution; it is only a step in your own growth in the Christian life, and in the gradual building up of God's people as a community of love, peace and faith. Your work now, in the words of the prayer above, is to 'proclaim to the world the wonderful works of God'.

READINGS, HYMNS, POEMS

The readings which follow are included in this book to help you reflect on God's creation, the world you live in, your hopes and fears, and on your faith. Hopefully they will help you to pray. There is no particular order in the selection of readings – simply choose what seems appropriate and read, slowly and reflectively, as much as seems helpful. When later you come back to the same reading you may be led to discover something quite fresh; there is always a new wine to be savoured. The sources of the readings are given in case you might like to read further.

GOD'S SPIRIT

In the beginning God created the heavens and the earth. Now the earth was a formless void, there was darkness over the deep, and God's Spirit hovered over the water.

Genesis 1:1-2

A PRAYER TO THE CREATOR

O our mother earth, O our father heaven,
we are your children.
The sacrifices you ask for
we offer with bent backs.
Weave us a garment of radiant sunlight,
the white dawn the warp,
the red evening the woof.
Let the murmuring rain be the fringe
and the rainbow the hem.
Weave us a garment of radiant sunlight.

We want to walk where the birds sing.
We want to walk through the green grass,
O our mother earth, O our father heaven.

An Indian prayer
quoted in Open Your Hearts, *by Huub Oosterhuis*

PRAISE OF GOD

The heavens proclaim the glory of God
and the firmament shows forth the work of his hands.
Day unto day takes up the story
and night unto night makes known the message.

No speech, no word, no voice is heard
yet their span extends through all the earth,
their words to the utmost bounds of the world.

There he has placed a tent for the sun;
it comes forth like a bridegroom coming from his tent,
rejoices like a champion to run its course.

At the end of the sky is the rising of the sun;
to the furthest end of the sky is its course.
There is nothing concealed from its burning heat.

Psalm 18 (19)

DIGGING

To-day I think
Only with scents, – scents dead leaves yield,
And bracken, and wild carrot's seed,
And the square mustard field;

78

Odours that rise
When the spade wounds the root of tree,
Rose, currant, raspberry, or goutweed,
Rhubarb or celery.

The smoke's smell, too,
Flowing from where a bonfire burns
The dead, the waste, the dangerous,
And all to sweetness turns.

It is enough
To smell, to crumble the dark earth,
While the robin sings over again
Sad songs of Autumn mirth.

Edward Thomas

THANKFULNESS

I thank you God for this most amazing
day: for the leaping greenly spirits of trees
and a blue true dream of sky: and for everything
which is natural which is infinite which is yes.

(i who have died am alive again today,
and this is the sun's birthday: this is the birth
day of life and of love and wings: and of the gay
great happening illimitably earth)

how should tasting touching hearing seeing
breathing any – lifted from the no
of all nothing – human merely being
doubt unimaginable You?

(now the ears of my ears awake and
now the eyes of my eyes are opened)

e. e. cummings

MY GOD AND KING

Let all the world in ev'ry corner sing,
    My God and King.

  The heav'ns are not too high,
  His praise may thither fly:
  The earth is not too low,
  His praises there may grow.

Let all the world in ev'ry corner sing,
    My God and King.

  The church with psalms must shout,
  No door can keep them out:
  But above all, the heart
  Must bear the longest part.

Let all the world in ev'ry corner sing,
    My God and King.
            George Herbert

PIED BEAUTY

Glory be to God for dappled things –
  For skies of couple-colour as a brinded cow;
    For rose-moles all in stipple upon trout that swim;
Fresh firecoal chestnut-falls; finches' wings;
  Landscape plotted and pieced – fold, fallow, and plough;
    And áll trádes, their gear and tackle and trim.

All things counter, original, spare, strange;
  Whatever is fickle, freckled (who knows how?)
    With swift, slow; sweet, sour; adazzle, dim;
He fathers-forth whose beauty is past change:
        Praise him.
           Gerard Manley Hopkins

BEHOLD THE MAN

Here is a man who was born in an obscure village, the child of a peasant woman. He worked in a carpenter's shop until he was thirty, and then for three years he was an itinerant preacher. He had no credentials but himself. While still a young man, the tide of popular opinion turned against him. His friends – the twelve men who had learned so much from him, and had promised him their enduring loyalty – ran away and left him. He went through a mockery of a trial; he was nailed upon a cross between two thieves; when he was dead, he was taken down and laid in a borrowed grave through the pity of a friend.

Yet I am well within the mark when I say that all the armies that ever marched, and all the parliaments that ever sat, and all the kings that ever reigned, put together, have not affected the life of man upon this earth as has this one solitary life.

Anonymous

FOLLOWING JESUS

Following Jesus
does not mean slavishly copying his life.
It means making his choice of life your own
starting from your own potential
and in the place where you find yourself.
It means living for the values
for which Jesus lived
and died.

It means following the path he took
and seeing things as he saw them.

If there is anything in which this life,
this way, can be expressed,
in which God has revealed himself most clearly,
it is the reality of love.
You are someone
only in as far as you are love,
and only what has turned to love in your life
will be preserved.

What love is
you can learn from Jesus.

He is the one who has loved most.
He will teach you to put the centre of yourself outside.
For no man has greater love
than he who lays down his life
for his friends.

Rule for a New Brother

OF FAMILIAR FRIENDSHIP WITH JESUS

When Jesus is present, all is well, and nothing seems difficult; but when Jesus is absent, everything is hard.

When Jesus does not speak within, consolation is little worth; but if Jesus speak but one word, we feel great consolation . . .

It is a great art to know how to converse with Jesus; and to know how to keep Jesus is great wisdom.

Be humble and peaceable, and Jesus will be with you. Be devout and calm, and Jesus will abide with you . . .

Without a friend, you cannot live well; and if Jesus be not your friend above all other friends, you shall indeed be sad and desolate.

Thomas à Kempis, The Imitation of Christ

YOU ARE EVERYWHERE

God, you are everywhere.
You are in the place and time
That we pronounce your name.
We have freely accepted
The choice that you have made of us
And that you continue to make
All the days of our lives.
We accept what we have learned of you
From Jesus Christ, your Son.
You are everywhere and always.
You are for all times.
And when we speak of you,
You use our lips
To be proclaimed to all creation.

François Chagneau, Stay With Us

THE FORM OF GOD

He bore the form of God;
yet he did not think likeness to God
just good fortune for himself alone.

He gave up everything
taking the form of a slave,
living life like other men.

As a man
he faced the worst;
obedience took him to his death.

So God raised him to the heights,
and gave him the name
above every name –

that at the name of Jesus
the living and dead
should hail him as Lord,

and everybody everywhere claim
'Jesus, God's Chosen Leader, is Lord!'
to the glory of God the Father.

Philippians 2:6-11, from Alan Dale, New World

DISCOVER YOURSELF

Every person must have a concern for self, and feel a
responsibility to discover his mission in life. God has
given each normal person a capacity to achieve some end.
True, some are endowed with more talent than others,
but God has left none of us talentless. Potential powers of
creativity are within us, and we have the duty to work
assiduously to discover these powers.

Martin Luther King

THE BOY
Lord,
I'm not a beast,
I'm just a boy.
Lion-like in my roar,
Camel-like in my up-turned nose.
I'm a head-burier, an all-ways turner,
Like a pirouetting ostrich-cum-starfish.
They tell me I'm prickly and docile in turn,
Part hedgehog, part lamb.
Flamboyant as a peacock,
Conformist as an ant.
I'm centipede, snail, swallow and gazelle.
Foot-dragger, house-humper, fly-away, care-free.
I chatter like a parrot,
Burrow like a mole,
Irritate like a flea,
Gnaw like a beaver,
Puff-up like a toad,
Fuss like a hen,
And weave complicated, fly-catching webs
        like a spider.
I'm all of these and none.
I'm a boy.
I'm an oyster with a pearl.
There is in me . . .
        an awakening, a strength,
        a joy, a purposefulness,
        a future, a life that knows no end.
God be praised for what I am,
And what I may become!
        AMEN   *David Konstant*

IN GOD'S CARE

Alone with none but thee, my God,
   I journey on my way;
What need I fear, when thou art near,
   O King of night and day?
More safe am I within Thy hand
Than if a host did round me stand.

Saint Columba

HOPE FOR THE FUTURE

You will forget your misery;
you will remember it as waters
that have passed away.
And your life will be brighter
than the noonday;

its darkness will be like the morning.
And you will have confidence,
because there is hope;
you will be protected
and take your rest in safety.
You will lie down
and none will make you afraid.   *Job 11:16-19*

THE CHANCE

Here I am, lonely in my mother's womb.
As I am lying here, I am wondering
Just whether to come out and see the bright world.
But maybe it is not a bright world,
It's maybe dull, but I can't tell
   if it is a dull world.

I will not be able to get back into the womb
   if it is dull.
It is just the chance I will have to take.

Timmy Crow, aged 11

A FLOWER HAS OPENED

A flower has opened in my heart . . .
What flower is this, what flower of spring,
What simple, secret thing?
It is the peace that shines apart,
The peace of daybreak skies that bring
Clear song and wild swift wing.
Heart's miracle of inward light,
What powers unknown have sown your seed
And your perfection freed? . . .
O flower within me wondrous white,
I know you only as my need
And my unsealed sight   *Siegfried Sassoon*

GROWING UP

Our knowledge is imperfect and our prophesying is
imperfect; but once perfection comes all imperfect things
will disappear. When I was a child, I used to talk like
a child, and think like a child, and argue like a child,
but now I am a man, all childish ways are put behind me.
Now we are seeing a dim reflection in a mirror; but then
we shall be seeing face to face. The knowledge that I
have now is imperfect; but then I shall know as fully as
I am known.   *1 Corinthians 13:9-12*

SELF ACCEPTANCE

I do not care much what others say and think about me. But there is one man's opinion which I value very much and that is the opinion of James Garfield. Others I need not think about. I can get away from them, but I have to be with him all the time. He is with me when I rise up and when I lie down; when I eat and talk, when I go out and come in. It makes a great difference whether he thinks well of me or not. *James Garfield*

THANKSGIVING

God who created me
Nimble and light of limb,
In three elements free,
To run, to ride, to swim;
Not when the sense is dim,
But now, from the heart of joy,
I would remember him;
Take the thanks of a boy. *H. C. Beeching*

DO WHAT IS WORTHWHILE

One last word. Give your minds to what is true and noble, right and clean, lovely and graceful. Wherever you find excellence – things really worth getting excited about – concentrate on them.

Philippians 4:8, from Alan Dale, New World

MY PARENTS

They gave me life
Can it be that what I am
Is theirs?
They cannot know my thoughts and hopes
And fears.

They gave me life,
Yet all I am is mine
Not theirs.
I've lived within myself alone
For years.

They gave me life
To run and think and grow my way
Not theirs.
Now I can give to them my happiness
Not tears.

Mark Vinten, aged 10

FORGIVE THEM FATHER, THEY KNOW NOT WHAT
THEY DO

(*This prayer was found in a concentration camp where
thousands of women and children had been killed.*)

Remember Lord,
   not just the men and women of good will
   but also those of ill will,
   not just our suffering,
   but also the fruits of this suffering –
     our comradeship, loyalty, humility,
     courage, generosity and greatness of heart,
   which has grown out of all this.

And when they come to judgment,
   let all the fruits that we have borne,
   be their forgiveness.   *Anonymous*

LATE HAVE I LOVED YOU!

Late have I loved you, O beauty so ancient and so new;
late have I loved you! For behold you were within me,
and I outside; and I sought you outside and in my
ugliness fell upon those lovely things that you have made.
You were with me and I was not with you. I was kept
from you by those things, yet had they not been in you,
they would not have been at all. You called and cried to
me and broke open my deafness: and you sent forth your
beams and shone upon me and chased away my blindness:
you breathed fragrance upon me, and I drew in my breath
and do now pant for you: I tasted you, and now hunger
and thirst for you: you touched me, and I have burned
for your peace.   *From* The Confessions of St Augustine

THE HOUND OF HEAVEN

O Lord, you search me and you know me,
you know my resting and my rising,
you discern my purpose from afar.
You mark when I walk or lie down,
all my ways lie open to you.

O where can I go from your spirit,
or where can I flee from your face?
If I climb the heavens, you are there.
If I lie in the grave you are there.

If I take the wings of the dawn
and dwell at the sea's furthest end,
even there your hand would lead me,
your right hand would hold me fast.

If I say: 'Let the darkness hide me
and the light around me be night,'
even darkness is not dark for you
and the night is as clear as the day.

For it was you who created my being,
knit me together in my mother's womb.
I thank you for the wonder of my being,
for the wonders of all your creation.

To me how mysterious your thoughts,
the sum of them not to be numbered!
If I count them, they are more than the sand:
to finish, I must be eternal, like you.

O search me, God, and know my heart.
O test me and know my thoughts.
See that I follow not the wrong path
and lead me in the path of life eternal.   *From Psalm 139*

THE PRAYER OF THE TORTOISE

A little patience,
O God,
I am coming.
One must take nature as she is!
It was not I who made her!
I do not mean to criticise
this house on my back –
it has its points –
but you must admit, Lord,
it is heavy to carry!
Still,
let us hope that this double enclosure,
my shell and my heart,
will never be quite shut to you.

Carmen Bernos de Gasztold, Prayers from the Ark

GOD'S ANSWER TO JOB

(The book of Job is the story of a good and rich man who suddenly lost all he had – wealth and health. He knows he is good and has done nothing to deserve such punishment. In the end he angrily asks God to write out his charges plainly, and answer Job's complaint. This is part of God's answer.)

Who darkens debate
    with ignorant talk?
Pull yourself together like a man
    and answer my questions.

You're a knowledgeable man –
    you must know!

Were you there
　　when I made the world –
settling its shape and size
　　and measuring it off?

Tell me –
where were its pillars sunk,
　　who laid the corner-stones
when the morning stars burst into song
　　and the hosts of heaven shouted aloud?
Where were you when the sea was born
　　tumbling in tumult from the earth –
blanketed in cloud
　　and swathed in fog?
when I fixed its final shores
　　like a bolted door:
'So far and no further –
　　here shall your surging stop!'?

Do you really think I'm unjust –
　　or are you just proving me wrong
　　　　to prove yourself right? . . .

From the Book of Job, Alan Dale, Winding Quest

OLD AGE

Age, gradually creeps
Overtakes and sleeps
Creaking old bones
Damp, lonely homes
Age
Shut up in a cage
Like animals, lonely and scared
With no one to care
No one there
Old Age.　　　　　*Sally Beale, aged 13*

MY HAND

My hand looks like a rake but only when I
bend my fingers.
And when I stretch my fingers they feel stiff
and if I loosen them they feel like tentacles
moving slowly.
My palm has a lot of rivers on it and they all
represent a pattern.
I would call the little rivers tributaries.
Now moving to the tips of my fingers I can see
a lot of circles like the rings of a tree when cut down.
Now I am touching the grass and it feels like the
soft bristles of a beard.
But now I am touching an old log and the
bark feels like an old man's wrinkles.
Now I am touching some velvet and it feels
like a small soft brush which when you touch
will move from side to side.
We can use our hands for building, giving,
helping, touching, smoothing, patting and waving.
But the most important thing is to give.

Leslie Scadding, aged 11

WHAT LOVE REALLY MEANS

I may speak all the languages of earth and heaven, but,
if I have no love in my heart, it's just like the old religions
with the din and noise of gong and cymbal. I may be a
'Man of God' and be able to understand and explain all
the wonders and secrets of God's Way; I may trust in
God with all my heart, trust him as Jesus told us to trust
him; but if I have no love in my heart, all this is worthless.
I may give everything I've got to feed hungry people;
I may be branded as a slave for what I believe; but if I

have no love in my heart, I get nothing at all out of it.

This is what love is like.

Love is never in a hurry, and is always kindness itself. It doesn't envy anybody at all, it never boasts about itself. It's never snobbish or rude or selfish. It doesn't keep on talking about the wrong things other people do; remembering the good things is happiness enough. It's tough – it can face anything. And it never loses trust in God, or in men and women; it never loses hope; and it never gives in.

Love holds good – everywhere, for everybody, for ever.

I Corinthians 13:1-13, from Alan Dale, New World

THE LORD IS RISEN

I rose early and went out into the fresh brilliant morning between 6 and 7 o'clock.

The sun had already risen some time but the grass was still white with the hoar frost. I walked across the Common between the Lady's Gates in the bright sunny quiet empty morning listening to the lark as he went up in an ecstasy of song into the blue unclouded sky and gave in his Easter morning hymn at Heaven's gate. Then came the echo and answer of earth as the Easter bells rang out their joy peals from the Church towers all round . . .

It was very sweet and lovely, the bright silent sunny morning, and the lark rising and singing alone in the blue sky, and then, suddenly, the morning air all alive with the music of sweet bells ringing for the joy of the Resurrection. 'The Lord is risen,' smiled the sun. 'The Lord is risen,' sang the lark. And the church bells in their joyous pealing answered from tower to tower, 'He is risen indeed.'

From Kilvert's Diary, *edited by William Plomer*

THE ASCENSION

In the days of his earthly ministry, only those could
speak to Jesus who came where he was. If he was in
Galilee, men could not find him in Jerusalem; if he was
in Jerusalem, men could not find him in Galilee. But his
Ascension means that he is perfectly united with God;
we are with him wherever we are present to God; and
that is everywhere and always. Because he is 'in heaven',
he is everywhere on earth; because he ascended, he is
here now.

Archbishop William Temple, Readings in St John's Gospel

THE WORD OF GOD

In the beginning was the Word:
the Word was with God
and the Word was God.
He was with God in the beginning.
Through him all things came to be,
not one thing had its being but through him.
All that came to be had life in him
and that life was the light of men,
a light that shines in the dark,
a light that darkness could not overpower.

The Word was the true light
that enlightens all men . . .
His own people did not accept him.
But to all who did accept him
he gave power to become children of God.
He was born of God himself.
The Word was made flesh,
he lived among us,
and we saw his glory,
the glory that is his as the only Son of the Father,
full of grace and truth.   *From John 1:1-14*